Kip Puterbaugh's
AVIARA
GOLF
ACADEMY

Fundamentals

of the

Golf Swing

INTRODUCTION

The objective of this instructional manual is to provide students of the **AVIARA GOLF ACADEMY** with a brief reminder of the swing principles that were taught in class.

This manual was intended to be as user friendly as possible. An attempt was made to state principles in a way that would apply to both right-handed and left-handed golfers. However, in some instances left-handed students will have to reverse the positions and moves described.

Enjoy the manual and good golfing.

THIS BOOK
BELONGS TO:

Aviara Golf Academy
7447 Batiquitos Drive
Carlsbad, CA 92011
(760) 438-4539
Email to: info@puterbaughgolf.com
AviaraGolfAcademy.com
Copyright © 1999, 2024 by Kip Puterbaugh
ISBN: 979-8-9892216-0-8
Printed in USA

FUNDAMENTALS OF THE GOLF SWING

TABLE OF CONTENTS

WEIGHT ON THE BALLS OF THE FEET

Good golf requires the proper stance and posture to be maintained to ensure that a full rotation of both the shoulders and hips can be made around the axis of the spine. **You must maintain your balance** to achieve the necessary rotation in a functional golf swing. As in all sports, the weight should be centered over the **balls of your feet**. The weight distribution will vary with how much weight is on each foot and the club type of shot you plan to make. Getting yourself in balance also requires **good posture** with your back straight and your head a continuation of your spine.

There is not one sport played in which the starting position is not on the balls of the feet. Golf is no exception. All too often, a golfer takes his stance, looks at the static (non-moving) ball, and creates a static address position. In this address, the golfer mistakenly places his weight on his heels, thinking he must be solely planted. Unfortunately, this places the body in a position that cannot properly rotate to transfer the weight on either the backswing or forward swing. If your spine is bent or curved upon address, your body cannot react in an athletic, balanced fashion and swing mistakes will multiply.

WEIGHT ON THE BALLS OF THE FEET

SPINE STRAIGHT

BALANCE

GRIP-NEUTRAL

The ideal hand position on the golf club is a **neutral position.** This means **neither hand is in a dominant position** of strength or weakness relative to the other hand.

A quick way to check your grip is to assume your address position and then cock your clubhead up until the clubhead has gone slightly past the position parallel to the ground. At this point, the **leading edge of the clubface should be pointing straight up and down**. If the club is pointing downward or to the left, your grip will generally be too strong. If your clubface points to the right of vertical, your grip will be too weak.

Grip Reminders: Your hands do not wrap around the grip. **Both hands should gently cradle the grip – place it into your fingers, not your palms.** Remember that your hands come down to the grip – never grip from underneath. Forcibly over-gripping the club from underneath places more pressure on the palms instead of the fingers. This overly tight or squeezed grip results in a loss of unity between the hands and, consequently, a loss of club control.

Once you have learned to grip the club properly, make it a habit to cock the club up and down to feel the balance and "squareness" of the clubface. Most good golfers do this as a matter of routine during their pre-shot setup. The club will feel much lighter in the neutral position: heavier when too open or closed. This drill can save a great deal of time in achieving a **constantly square clubface at address**.

The butt end of the grip must be underneath the pad or the "fatty" part of the left hand. If the grip is allowed to move toward the center of your palm, you will have to hold the club too tightly to maintain control. If your glove shows excessive wear in this area, there is a good chance you need to move the grip further back on the pad.

GRIP-NEUTRAL CONTINUED

PAD ON TOP
OF GRIP

LEFT HAND POSITION

THUMB AND FOREFINGER CLOSE TOGETHER

INNER PORTION OF THE THUMB LEFT OF CENTER LINE

RIGHT HAND POSITION:

THUMB AND FOREFINGER CLOSE TOGETHER

INNER PORTION OF THE THUMB RIGHT OF CENTER LINE

With this neutral grip, there are many points to check to ensure your hands are on the club correctly. From the golfer's point of view, notice in the photo (from the top down):

Trigger finger of the right hand

No gap between thumb and forefinger of right hand

"V" of right thumb and forefinger pointing toward the right ear and shoulder

Right thumb position slightly left of the center of the grip

Three knuckles of left hand visible

Cupped or angled position between left forearm/wrist and the top of the left hand

Ability for both the right and left wrists to "hinge" upward while the clubface remains square

Left hand placement relative to the inner thigh of the left leg

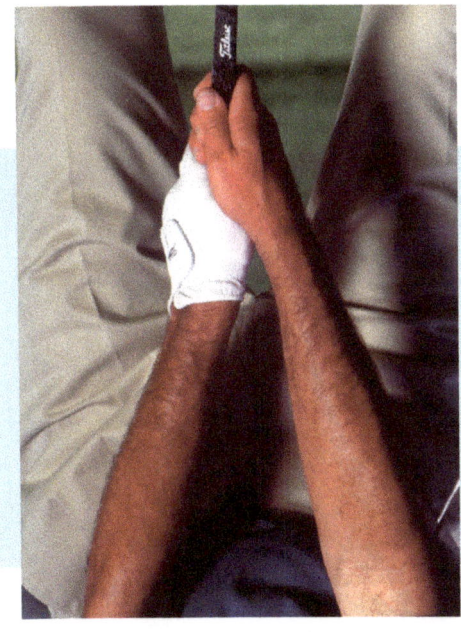

7

TENSION –
HANDS, ARMS & SHOULDERS

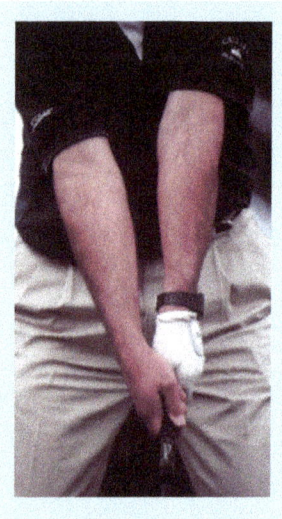

TIGHT ELBOWS AND HYPEREXTENDED ARMS RESULT IN TOO MUCH INNER ARM BEING VISIBLE

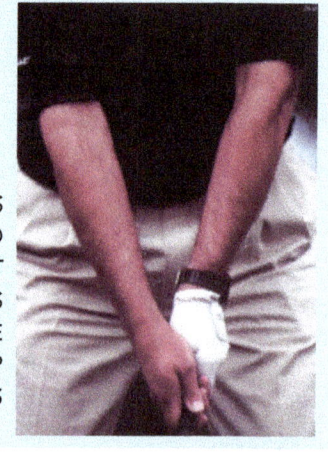

ELBOWS RELAXED AND CORRECT ARM ANGLES SHOW MORE OF THE TOP OF THE ARMS

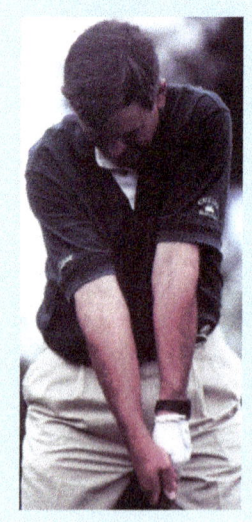

NECK AND SHOULDERS VERY TIGHT WITH NO FREEDOM OF MOVEMENT FROM THIS POSITION

SHOULDERS AND NECK MUSCLES RELAXED ALLOWING FREEDOM OF MOVEMENT

TENSION –
HANDS, ARMS & SHOULDERS

If I could give all golfers one tip, it would be based on a quote from George Knudsen's book, ***You Have to Give Up Control to Gain Control***. This sums it up because the average golfer makes the mistake of gripping the club too tightly, trying to control the clubface through the impact area. You must give up this control to **let centrifugal force square up the clubface**. It has been proven in all cultures around the world that when humans face stressful situations, they tend to tighten up, tensing the muscles in the hands, arms, shoulders and neck. Unfortunately, when confronted with golf, people often react with stress, drastically reducing their ability to control the swing with the large muscles of the legs, hip and back.

Golf is a challenging sport because **you start from a static position** and are not reacting to a target or ball moving toward you. That contributes to a critical error: getting too involved in merely making contact with the ball versus hitting it toward **your real target – where you want the ball to go**. Your success in hitting quality golf shots may require a change in priorities to avoid that tendency to make the *golf ball* your target. The more you consider the ball your primary target, the more tension you create in trying to hit it. Focus on the actual target and remember that **the ball is merely getting in the way of the clubhead swinging out**.

"You have to give up control to gain control."

– George Knudsen

ALIGNMENT

Feet, knees & shoulders parallel left

Clubface toward target

Upper spine slightly right of vertical

Spine angle slightly right of vertical

ALIGNMENT

All golfers should constantly check their alignment to ensure they are not developing bad habits in aligning their feet, knees, hips and shoulders. Most amateurs do not spend enough time working with their alignment. Poor alignment is where, quite often, they will find the root of their problems.

You may have noticed that professional golfers often practice with "alignment clubs" placed on the ground. If you watch amateurs practice, it is rare to see alignment clubs. Why do the world's best players use these aids for practice? The answer is that they know through experience how easy it is to get out of alignment. One hour of practicing out of alignment is one hour of creating swing faults. There is nothing more frustrating than wasting time. So, when you practice, follow the prescribed drills to achieve proper alignment.

The function of the address position is to prepare you to have a balanced athletic platform in parallel alignment with the target, allowing you to build up energy to transfer to the target, with the ball merely getting in the way of that energy.

FUNDAMENTAL #1
INITIATE WITH THE BODY

As the motion of the swing begins, we should remember the overall goal of the golf swing, which is for the clubhead to achieve *centrifugal force*. Remember that centrifugal force originates from the *center*; therefore, **you must start the clubhead in motion from the body, not the hands and arms.**

CLUB STAYS
CENTERED
WITH BODY
THROUGHOUT
ROTATION OF HIPS
& SHOULDERS

AS BODY TURNS,
ARMS STAY IN
FRONT OF TORSO

FUNDAMENTAL #1
INITIATE WITH THE BODY CONTINUED

One significant error the amateur golfer makes is initiating the golf swing from the hands and arms. **Ideally, it should feel like the clubhead is an extension of your belly button**. As you move into the backswing, you want to feel like the clubhead is moving in sync with the rotation of your chest. As you begin to move your chest to the right, your upper body or shoulders will feel the majority of the movements. This does not mean that your hips cannot be involved. Your hips need to work properly to allow your shoulders to rotate on a level plane across your body. Remember, the chair drill training from class was an exercise in getting your hips to turn properly instead of sliding back laterally away from the target. **The primary goal as you start the backswing is the early involvement of your torso rotating toward your back foot and your arms swinging freely from your body in response to your body turning**.

Remember that you are not trying to turn your shoulders under your chin but across your body. Any attempt to go under usually causes the left shoulder to drop down, which will correspondingly raise your right hip up and therefore prevent you from making the proper rotation.

Another area of concern in the initial backswing rotation is the rotation of your eyes. The videos about the world's best players showed how they let their heads move slightly laterally and their eyes rotate around to allow for the proper level of rotation of the shoulders. If you do not let your eyes rotate at the start of the backswing, there is a very good chance you will never make the proper shoulder and hip turn. The eyes do play a pivotal part in the rotation away from the ball. **As you rotate your eyes, your view of the ball will be with the peripheral vision of your left eye**.

Look at the pictures and practice in front of a mirror to learn this all-important part of the gold swing.

PROPER SHOULDER ROTATION

You will execute proper rotation if you adhere to Fundamental #1: Initiate With the Body. It is helpful to understand that the rotation of the upper body has to happen much sooner in the backswing than most realize. You are in the correct position when your left hand has reached the waist-high level on the first half of your backswing. The photo shows that the right shoulder is not visible because it rotates behind the neck. A common mistake is to lead with the arms so that at the halfway point, most of the right shoulder is still visible by someone facing the golfer. This error results in excessive arm movement at the top of the backswing. If you move your arms too quickly in relation to your body rotation, you set yourself up for a swing that is *out of rhythm*. To help set the initial rhythm, **it should feel like the clubhead is traveling at the same speed as your chest or belly button rotation around the axis of your spine**.

RIGHT ARM
ON TOP OF LEFT

LEGS STABLE

THE CLUBHEAD REMAINS OUTSIDE THE HANDS

At address you can create two parallel lines. One goes through the clubhead and is aimed directly at the target. The lower line runs parallel to the target and is directly below the hands. **The line closest to your feet is the *inside* line, and the line through the clubhead is the *outside* line**. As the clubhead approaches the parallel-to-the-ground position, it stays to the outside of the hands. As previously stated, a major problem of the amateur is to move the club too quickly with the hands and arms on the backswing. This invariable leads to the clubhead going *inside* the hands in the beginning stages of the backswing. Suppose the club goes to the inside too quickly. In that case, you end up with one of two results: getting the club *too flat* or *low* if you rotate your body with the *inside* move of the club. Or, if you don't rotate your body, you will be forced to lift the club into an extremely upright position. This will not occur if you adhere to Fundamental #1: Initiate With the Body. If the clubhead stays *outside* your hands, you can rotate your body to the conclusion of the backswing, and the club will stay on the correct plane.

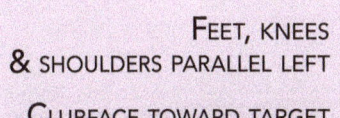

FEET, KNEES & SHOULDERS PARALLEL LEFT

CLUBFACE TOWARD TARGET

CLUBHEAD OUTSIDE OF HANDS

CLUBHEAD ON PLANE

15

WEIGHT TRANSFER
PROPER SPINE ANGLE

Proper weight transfer in the backswing is one of the most misunderstood maneuvers of the golf swing. As a result of the misunderstanding, it is rarely executed properly. Even beginners understand that a weight shift is necessary to develop a powerful and consistent golf swing. Unfortunately, most golfers shift their weight laterally. Proper weight shift results when your hips and shoulders rotate correctly. Focus on your spin. In the photo, notice the angle of the spine from the back. The line from the hips to

RIGHT ARM
ON TOP OF LEFT

LEGS STABLE

BODY TURNING,
CLUB STAYS IN
SEQUENCE WITH
BODY TURN

ARMS COMFORTABLY
EXTENDED FROM BODY

the shoulders points slightly to the right of vertical. Your spine rests in this position because your right hand is lower than your left in the address and gripping of the club. That lowers your right shoulder slightly and, therefore, tilts the spine slightly to the right. Throughout the backswing, your goal is to keep your spine angle pointing to the right of vertical.

The most common mistake we see at the **AVIARA GOLF ACADEMY** is students trying to shift their weight laterally, causing their hips to slide to the right. When the hips slide to the right, the base of the spine follows, causing your spine to point to the left of vertical. This sequence of events makes it impossible to rotate your shoulders. The only way you can effectively rotate your shoulders is to keep your hips from sliding laterally. Your right hip (for right-handed golfers) should merely move backward as your shoulders rotate into a position where your chest is almost over your rear foot.

You can understand the average player's dilemma; in their attempt to create a weight shift, they end up putting their body into a reverse shift because of the change in spine angle.

Practice this:

1. Watch your reflection in a mirror or window and check to see that you are creating a "V," as shown in the photo.

2. Visually draw a vertical line perpendicular to the ground, starting from your left or lead hip.

3. Then imagine a line that is parallel to the angle of your back.

These two lines form the "V." Most amateurs do not create that "V." If your backswing does not, your spine is leaning the wrong way at the top of your backswing, resulting in excessive arm movement and inconsistent shot patterns.

Your body must be actively involved in creating the proper weight shift and, consequently, the speed of your arms and body, leaving you in a good position at the completion of the backswing. Try to practice these initial moves with the aid of a mirror, window or video camera.

LEFT ARM ON PLANE

The correct placement of your left arm at the top of the backswing is performed easily if your position is correct the halfway point. The desired position is with the left arm bisecting the angle of the shoulders and crossing the top of the right shoulder. The ideal position will allow you to easily get your club on the plane early in the downswing.

Two ways you can misplace your left arm during the backswing are: too far below the right shoulder, and too far above the right shoulder.

CLUBFACE SQUARE

LEFT ARM PARALLEL
WITH THE SWING PLANE

RIGHT KNEE FLEXED

NOSE OVER LEFT SHOULDER,
RIGHT AND HIP INNER PORTION
OF RIGHT KNEE

LEFT ARM ON PLANE CONTINUED

The left-arm-below-the-right-shoulder position results from the golfer whose hands and arms move too quickly at the start of the backswing. This overuse results in the initial path of the backswing going too far inside the swing path. After the club has traveled on the inside path, the golfer then adds some rotation of the hips and shoulders, resulting in a position in which the left arm is *below plane*. If you then drew a line through that club shaft and the left arm, it would be pointing far above the position of the ball. Once in this position, the golfer will be forced to lift this arm and club in order to make contact with the ball. That lifting of the club shaft and arm results in a swing path that is too far outside. This will force the slice on the longer shots and pulls with the shorter clubs. While the position of below plane would be great for hitting an outside fastball in baseball, the plane must have a more vertical position to prepare to hit a golf ball. That is not to say you should never swing a golf club like a baseball bat. On the contrary, the golf swing is nothing more than a baseball swing on a different arc. As a matter of fact, many professional baseball players play golf very well because the two sports are so similar in motion. **NOTE:** Many golfers suffer from "the slice" and know that to get rid of it, they have to make their club travel on an *inside out* path of the forward swing. Unfortunately, in trying to create the inside path, they take their backswing too far inside, forcing the lift of their arms and creating the outside in the path they were trying to eliminate.

The primary cause of your left arm going too high above your shoulder on the backswing is an attempt to keep your head too stationary and, therefore, anchoring your entire body form moving. When the torso is frozen with fear of head movement, the arms again initiate the backswing, with the hips and shoulders not participating. This results in your arms running into your torso at about the chest area, causing the position of your left arm to be *above plane*. From this position at the top of the backswing, the golfer can only throw his arms and hands down to the ball with no participation from the torso. If he tried to use his legs, hips and shoulders from this position, the results would be a whiff or topping of the ball.

MAINTAINING THE "V" – SPINE ANGLE CONSTANT, AWAY FROM THE TARGET

The importance of the angle of the spine pointing to the right of vertical through the backswing cannot be stressed enough. **To create the "V," you cannot allow your hips to slide laterally**, as that will cause them to run slightly back as your shoulders make the required rotation around to your right. When executed correctly, the "V" will be formed. Remember the line drawn perpendicular to the ground starting at the outside edge of your left hip, plus the line parallel to your back? These two lines should form a "V." If you have moved your hips laterally or have not turned your shoulders far enough away from the target, the resulting lines are perpendicular. The goal of the proper spine angle is to position your body in a manner that makes you feel natural to initiate the forward swing with the lower body – much like a baseball player would initiate his swing with the forward stepping of his lead foot.

THE "V"

SPINE ANGLE TO THE RIGHT

HIPS LEVEL

WEIGHT CENTERED ON TOP INSIDE OF THE REAR FOOT (BALL OF FOOT)

Much of a proper and consistent golf swing is based on maintaining good balance. As your shoulders rotate to the right on your backswing, your right leg retains its original flex and the balance of the body weight is centered over the top inside of the rear foot. **There are two phrases commonly used in teaching golf that are often misapplied:**

1. **Keep your weight on the inside of your rear foot**. Although this is essentially correct, it often results in a reverse weight shift. This happens because the player resists any weight transfer to the rear foot by bracing rigidly against their left. As a result, a rotation away from the ball is made, and the shoulders stay over the lead foot (left foot for right-handed players) instead of rotating to a position more over the rear foot. The reason to focus on the *top* of the inside of the rear foot is to allow you to transfer the weight *over and on top of your foot*, whereas keeping your weight on just the inside most often results in the reverse weight shift.

2. **Transfer your weight to the heel of your rear foot**. This, too, can lead to poor results. If you work on transferring your weight onto the heel of your rear foot, your rear leg will straighten up, throwing off your balance. Ideally, your weight should feel centered, without too much on your toes or heels. You will feel your weight on your thigh muscle, through your calf muscle and on top of the inside portion of your rear foot.

SPINE ANGLE TO THE RIGHT

RIGHT HIP INSIDE RIGHT FOOT

STABLE LOWER BODY

21

PROPER SEQUENCE

In creating the proper motions of the backswing, **the sequence and timing of those motions are critical to your shot consistency**, especially at the time of change in direction.

When completing the backswing and beginning the forward swing, remember the importance of your arms trailing your body's lead. As in the examples of throwing a ball or hitting a baseball, the motion always starts with the body. Imagine the energy starting from the ground and working up through the body. A boxer using an uppercut is a good example of the energy coming from the

ARMS PASSIVE

NO TENSION IN SHOULDERS

HIPS INSIDE RIGHT FOOT

RIGHT THIGH ANGLED INWARD TO HIP SOCKET

ground up. Focusing on working from the ground up will slow down your hands and arms at the change of direction. Suppose your arms act too quickly at the top of the backswing. In that case, centrifugal force will be lost, and the club will invariably come from outside your swing plane, resulting in diminished power and clubface control.

For proper sequence, remember **whatever gets to the top of the backswing first will start down first**. If your hands and arms are too active, they will get to the top of your backswing before your body has completed the necessary turn and weight transfer. Thus, your arms will reach the top of the backswing first and, therefore, start the downswing first, creating an improper sequence of motion.

The proper sequence of motion is achieved when the correct body turn and weight transfer have occurred before your arms and hands have finished the backswing. This allows your body to change direction from the backswing to the forward swing. If you study the processional in slow motion, you will notice their club shaft continues on its way back as their body has started to transfer weight to their front foot.

Your proper sequence is achieved when you can obtain the proper timing and tempo for your swing. In studying the great players, you will notice that they all have distinct tempos. For example, Ben Hogan had a tempo that appeared to be very quick, whereas Jack Nicklaus appears very slow. However, when you study their swings, you can see that their sequence of motion or change of direction at the top of their backswings are identical. In both cases, the body (not the hands and arms) wins the race to the top of the backswing.

Whatever gets to the top of the backswing first, will start down first.

INITIATE WITH THE BODY, FEET, HIPS & SHOULDERS

To allow your body to start the forward swing, you must have the proper rotation and weight transfer to feel natural starting the forward swing with your lower body. This will occur if you have created the "V" in your spine angle (as was stressed at the Start of the Backswing section.) Also, your arms must be relaxed enough that they do not get actively involved in the transition between the end of the backswing and the initiation of the forward swing. If your arms have too much tension, it will transfer to your hands. Your forward swing will start from your hands and arms, not your body.

WEIGHT SHIFTS
OVER BALL
OF LEFT FOOT

INITIATE WITH THE BODY, FEET, HIPS & SHOULDERS CONTINUED

To help your body start the forward swing, try to achieve these feelings:

Feel your left hip transfer your weight over as it begins to rotate around and to the left. During the transfer, your weight should be going onto the ball of your lead foot. This shift toward the target will be a slight lateral bump of your hips, generally about two inches. As your weight shifts, your hips will start to turn. **It is important to remember the correct sequence, "shift and turn."** You never want it to be turn and shift.

You can also initiate the forward swing from the right side. **As you push off with your right foot while transferring your weight onto your left foot, you will feel a pushing motion that causes your hips to shift your weight, and your left hip will start to rotate around to the left**. As your right foot pushes off, you will also feel the left quadriceps muscle begin to straighten. Once your right side has started this motion, you will feel your right shoulder rotate your weight *onto and around to* a high position of the torso. Your arms should be partially around, with your right arm slightly above your left shoulder.

Feel your left hip transfer your weight over as it begins to rotate around to the left.

CLUB AND ARMS FOLLOW FROM BEHIND BODY MOTION

CLUB STAYS
BEHIND THE
BODY AND
ON THE PLANE

BACK OF LEFT
HAND & CLUB
SHAFT FORM
STRAIGHT LINE

CLUB AND ARMS FOLLOW FROM BEHIND BODY MOTION CONTINUED

Check the position of your arms and clubhead halfway down to the impact area. When your wrist has reached the waist-high position, your clubhead and arms should still be behind your body. Your club and arms will stay behind your body because they should have been inactive during the first half of the downswing. The hips and shoulders must perform this portion of the swing. After your hips have transferred your weight to your left side, they continue to rotate and transfer your weight up and onto your left foot and leg.

The major mistake of the amateur in this portion of the swing is overuse of their hands and arms, with very little use of the bigger muscles. If you make that error, the position you will likely to see at the waist-high spot is your arms and club in front of your body. This overuse of hands and arms creates an outside-to-inside path of the clubhead, resulting in a downswing path that is much too steep or descending. This downward and descending arc is very common and results in many inconsistencies in their ball striking.

For better ball-striking, key on a shallow approach to impact

TWO CHEEKS

This term refers to the position where both cheeks are visible at the impact position when executing a full swing. With a professional caliber player, when their lower body rotates, their shoulders also have rotated to where they point to the left of the target line at impact. This position, in which your body is to the left of the target line, is critical for several reasons. First, when your body has aligned to the left, your arms and hands have a free pathway to gain maximum speed.

Second, it allows centrifugal force to stay in effect because your body is pulling on the outer edge of the arc, delaying the acceleration of the club head allowing you to **"swing through the ball" instead of "at the ball."**

SHOULDERS STAY
SLIGHTLY LEFT

TWO CHEEKS

Try to visualize other sports that involve throwing or hitting, and consider the moment of contact or release of the throw. In baseball, to hit the ball effectively, you naturally have your body open to the left at the ball's impact. And when throwing a ball, whether a baseball or a football, your body would again be open to the intended line of flight. If you are a tennis player, consider how your body is aligned at impact on a top spin, forehand volley. Golf is no exception; **the arms must follow the lead and rotation of the torso**.

Perhaps you have read instruction articles that say that at impact, you should try to be as close as possible to your address position. If that were true, then in the examples of other sports, you would see the bodies lined parallel with their target line, not to the left. If you have played any of those sports, you realize how poorly you would bat, throw, or hit if your body was not allowed to rotate at impact. It has been stressed throughout this manual that overusing hands and arms results in the body not having time to rotate and clear the path to the impact point. The amateur is successful at returning to a position similar to their address because of their overuse of arms and hands. Having to force the hands through because the body is in the way causes the clubhead to lose speed rapidly, and the angle of descent toward the ball will be too vertical or steep.

The ideal feeling at impact is the culmination of the club coming from behind your body rotation when your weight has transferred to the ball of your lead foot and your body has cleared out of the way to allow the clubhead to accelerate through to the target.

Swing "through the ball"
instead of "at the ball."

FORWARD SWING

YOUR HEAD MOVES UP AND OUT

In the properly executed follow-through, your head will rise from the impact position and travel toward the target. One phrase all golfers should forget is "keep your head down." This is very likely the most dangerous swing tip in golf. Your head should not interfere with the energy that has been generated by the rotation of your torso. Your head should stay on top of your shoulders as they swing around to your lead side. If you overemphasize keeping your head down, it acts as an anchor, preventing anything below it from moving, thus impeding centrifugal force and pushing your arms up into your body. In an interview with two old-time teachers, Harvey Pennick and Norman Von Nida, who taught many of the great players in the game, the interviewer asked what was and what wasn't important in the swing. They both immediately answered,

BODY ROTATES AROUND & UP ONTO LEFT FOOT

"I can tell you very quickly what is *not* important in the golf swing, and that is trying to keep your head down. Show me a golfer, trying to keep his head down, and I will show you a poor *golfer*." If keeping your head down was the cure for the golf swing, all golf instructors would be out of business. Every golfer in the world has been told to keep his head down, but their swing never gets any better when they do that. Recently, the National Golf Foundation conducted a survey and received some interesting results. The average beginning golfer, in their first year of playing, improves on a steady basis. After their first year of golf, they rarely show any further improvement in their game. This indicates that the average golfer does not work on the proper fundamentals.

As previously discussed, golf is the only sport where the ball is not moving while you try to hit it. In all other sports, you must watch it in order to hit it. Since the golf ball isn't moving, there are numerous blind golfers who never miss. They *never* miss the ball. In fact, the National Blind Champion usually shoots under 80, and one year, the winner shot a 77. This tells you that keeping your head down is not an essential ingredient of the proper swing.

Over the years, many students at the **AVIARA GOLF ACADEMY** were confident they looked up at the point of impact. We asked these students to hit some balls with the video camera running and told them to let us know when they hit the ball while they looked up. Usually, within several swings, they say, "that was it, I looked up on that one." When the video is played back, they see otherwise.

Your head is not the pivot point of the golf swing – your feet are. When you transfer your weight from foot to foot, your head travels where your body takes it during the swing. Your head moves as your weight is displaced while loading and unloading it during the swing. Remember that your weight is transferred from foot to foot throughout the proper rotation of your body. Your head goes back and forth and up and down as your body carries your head.

SHORT GAME

The goals in executing shots around the green are to judge the distance you need to hit the ball and vary the elevation or trajectory of the ball flight as called for by the various conditions and slopes around the green. To be able to change the elevation or trajectory of the ball flight, you should understand three types of shots:

- **The Pitch & Run**
- **The Standard Pitch**
- **The Lob**

LEADING EDGE

FLANGE

BUTT END

TO UNDERSTAND THOSE THREE TYPES OF SHOTS, YOU SHOULD KNOW THE FOLLOWING TERMS:

Center: Your sternum is the center of the swing arc for all golf swings Where you place your sternum in relation to your body will significantly determine where the bottom of your swing arc will occur.

Butt End of the Club: All golf clubs have two ends. The clubhead is one end, and the grip side of the club is called the Butt End of the Club.

Clubface Loft / Delofted, Standard (Given) and Lofted: With the Standard Loft, the clubface is in the address position with the butt end of the club directly on top of the clubhead. If the butt end of the club is ahead of the clubface, the club is **delofted**. If the butt end of the club is behind the clubface at address, the club is **lofted**.

Leading Edge of the Club: This is the front edge of the clubface where it joins with the front edge of the sole or bottom of the club.

Flange: This is the back end of the sole.

General Rule: Wherever you place the butt end of the club, your weight should follow. If the club is straight up and down, your weight should be distributed equally between your feet. If the butt end of the club goes forward, so should your weight. If the butt end goes behind the ball, your weight should be more on the rear foot.

Goal: At impact, you should try to return to the position in which you started your shot with regard to the butt end of the club and clubface.

THE PITCH & RUN

SHOULDERS LEVEL

CENTER FORWARD

BUTT END FORWARD

ADDRESS POSITION OF THE PITCH & RUN:

Stance – square to slightly open

Ball placement – opposite the big toe of your rear foot

Width of stance – relatively narrow, approximately five inches between the heels

Butt end of the club – forward of the ball by two-to-three inches

Clubface – delofted from the club's given loft

Body center – three inches in front of the ball, shoulders level with sensation of looking back at the ball

Weight distribution – 75 percent on the front foot

Bottom of the swing arc – two-to-three inches in front of the ball

Clubface contact point at impact –leading edge of the club

Club selection – 7 iron through sand wedge

THE PITCH & RUN CONTINUED

This shot is used when the green side situation calls for a low-flight trajectory that will cause the ball to roll on the ground the majority of the distance to the hole. You use this shot when the pin is sufficiently far back from the edge of the green that you can easily "carry" the ball onto the surface and allow the ball to roll to the hole. You select this shot if the green you are "pitching to" is sloped upward, and you need to get the ball rolling up. If it is a split-level green and the pin is on the top level, you would also select this shot. You should use this shot whenever possible. Many amateurs hit a high type of approach to the green when it is unnecessary.

EXECUTION OF THE PITCH & RUN

With the combination of address positions in mind, you are ready to hit this type of descending-arc shot. Since with this shot your chosen club is in a deflofted position, it is not necessary to hit it as hard as the other pitches. On the backswing, keep your weight on the front foot without any real feeling of weight transfer toward the rear foot. At the address position, you start with the butt end of the club ahead of the ball and maintain this relationship through to the point past impact.

Notice the feeling that the clubhead never passes the hands. The only way to generate this feeling is with a very active rotation of the shoulders and a firm left wrist through impact. A common error of amateurs is to limit body motion around the greens, and to try to help the ball get into the air. If you do not keep your shoulders active and rotating toward your lead foot, the clubhead will flip past your hands too early in the forward swing, ruining the relationship of the butt end of the club staying ahead of the clubface. When this relationship breaks down, you add loft back onto the club because the clubhead passes the butt end. This error will cause the shot to go higher than intended and will not allow the ball to roll to the target.

THE PITCH & RUN CONTINUED

ADDRESS PITCH & RUN

SHOULDERS LEVEL

CENTER FORWARD

BUTT END FORWARD

TOP OF BACKSWING

SHOULDERS LEVEL

CENTER FORWARD

BUTT END FORWARD

IMPACT

HIPS AND SHOULDERS
ROTATE AND
TRANSFER WEIGHT

KNUCKLES OF LEFT
HAND STAY DOWN

FINISH

EYES "TARGET-AWARE"

BODY FACING TARGET

WEIGHT FORWARD

THE STANDARD PITCH

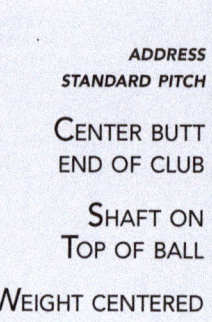

ADDRESS STANDARD PITCH

CENTER BUTT END OF CLUB

SHAFT ON TOP OF BALL

WEIGHT CENTERED

ADDRESS POSITION OF THE STANDARD PITCH:

Stance – slightly open of the target line

Ball placement – center of the stance

Width of stance – approximately six-to-eight inches between the inside of the heels

Butt end of the club – straight up and down

Clubface – a standard or given loft

Body center – directly over the ball, with the nose directly above the sternum

Weight distribution – equally distributed between the two feel

Bottom of the swing arc – directly under the ball

Clubface contact point at impact – the flange, causing a "skid effect"

Club selection – sand wedge

THE STANDARD PITCH CONTINUED

This shot is used when you need to elevate the ball on a higher trajectory than The Pitch & Run. If the pin is a little closer to the edge of the green, or the green is sloping away from you, then the Standard Pitch will give you a higher and softer landing or approach.

EXECUTION OF THE STANDARD PITCH

To execute this shot properly, you need to rotate your body on both the backswing and forward swing. Grip pressure must stay light, and as you start to hit shots with more loft around the greens, your wrist has to "cock" the clubhead up earlier in the backswing. When hitting lofted shots, your goal is to get the club shaft and the lead arm to form a 90-degree angle. Once you have rotated the center (torso & shoulders) away on the backswing with this 90-degree angle, the sensation should be that the club head drops softly back to the bottom of the swing arc as your body rotates through to a balanced finish. Incorporate your turn, drop and turn drill to help learn the proper feeling of rotation and the club "dropping" and coming back up without excessive grip pressure.

Remember that success or failure on these shots is not dictated by how still you keep your head or how long you keep your eyes on the ball. You need to work on trying to "feel the ground," and learn how to have the clubhead bottom out at the position predetermined with the starting position. An easy way to start building a sense of the "bottom of your swing arc" is to close your eyes and lightly tap the ground with your clubhead. As you tap, you will start to feel your grip tension lighten and feel the weight of the clubhead. Then, take a swing and try to have the clubhead thump the ground at the bottom as you swing into your follow-through. After a little practice, repeat this drill with your eyes open. After a few practice swings, try hitting a few balls. Start by tapping the ground with your clubhead and let the club swing on its arc as the ball **merely gets in the way of the swinging club** and torso.

THE STANDARD PITCH CONTINUED

ADDRESS
STANDARD PITCH

CENTER BUTT
END OF CLUB

SHAFT ON
TOP OF BALL

WEIGHT CENTERED

TOP OF BACKSWING

SHOULDERS
TURNING

90 DEGREE ANGLE
WRIST COCKING

LEGS STABLE

IMPACT

HIPS AND
SHOULDERS
ROTATING LEFT

FLANGE CONTACT

FINISH

WEIGHT BALANCED
ON FRONT FOOT

ARMS RELAXED
AND BY LEFT SIDE
OF TORSO

THE LOB

ADDRESS LOB

SPINE TILTED BACK

BALL FORWARD
BUTT END BEHIND BALL

ADDRESS POSITION OF THE LOB:

Stance – slightly open

Ball placement – opposite the inside heel of your forward foot

Width of stance – approximately eight inches between the insides of the heels

Butt end of the club – behind the ball by about one to two inches

Clubface – lofted, with more than given loft

Body center – behind the ball by about one to two inches

Weight distribution – 55% on the front foot

Bottom of the swing arc – one to two inches behind the ball based upon how you set the butt end of the club and center at address

Clubface contact point at impact – The flange should be the only contact with the ground

Club selection – sand wedge

THE LOB CONTINUED

The Lob is used when you need maximum elevation on your pitch so the ball will land softly with very little forward roll. You need this shot when you have a bunker to pitch over, and the pin is located on the near side of the green. You also need this shot if you have a tree or other obstacle in front of you. With proper execution of The Lob, you can go over the obstacle and get to the green. This shot requires a descent cushion of grass to have the opportunity to execute the shot, and it cannot be performed off hard pan or very tight lies.

EXECUTION OF THE LOB

The execution of The Lob is identical to the Standard Pitch. The only difference is the address position. Concentrate on letting the clubhead release past the hands, with the flange "skidding" on the turf. The clubhead cannot release over as in a normal swing. The release is more of a hinging of the wrist to allow the clubface to stay skyward through the ball.

The most common mistake we see in the execution of this shot is an attempt to lift and help the ball up into the air. This is a major error because, in the attempt to lift the ball, you move your center back away from the target. This moves the bottom of the arc too far behind the ball, causing the club to ascend up into the middle of the ball. You must keep your body rotating around and onto the front foot as you allow the club to release past your hands, returning to the angles you started with at address. You should allow for the added loft of the club you started with to get the ball up into the air. Do not attempt to help the ball up.

THE LOB CONTINUED

ADDRESS LOB

SPINE TILTED BACK

BALL FORWARD
BUTT END BEHIND BALL

TOP OF BACKSWING

BODY TURNED

SLIGHTLY MORE WRIST COCK

THE LOB CONTINUED

IMPACT

BODY TURNING

CLUB PASSING HANDS

FLANGE SKIDDING

FINISH

WEIGHT ON LEFT FOOT

EYES "TARGET-AWARE"

45

THE CHIP SHOT

ADDRESS CHIP

HANDS FORWARD

LEFT ARM RELAXED

BALL BACK

SHOULDERS LEVEL

ADDRESS POSITION OF THE CHIP SHOT

Stance – square to slightly open

Ball placement – opposite the big toe of your rear foot. (Right foot for right handers.)

Width of stance – relatively narrow, with between three to five inches between the heels.

Butt end of the club – forward of the ball by about three inches.

Body center – three inches in front of the ball, shoulders level with the sensation of looking back at the ball

Weight distribution – 75% on front foot at address, no shift on the backswing, and 90% on front foot at finish

Bottom of the swing arc – three inches in front of the ball

Clubface contact point at impact – leading edge of the club

Club selection – 6 iron through the sand wedge

THE CHIP SHOT CONTINUED

The Chip Shot is used when you are within approximately 15 feet of the greens edge. You have ample room to hit a lower trajectory shot and carry onto the green, and let the ball roll the remainder of the distance to the hole. **The Chip Shot is always used when attempting to get a low, running type of shot.** If you happen to be within 15 feet of the green, but the pin is close to the edge of the green, and the green slope is downhill, then you would be forced to hit a Standard Pitch or Lob. The technique of hitting the Chip is virtually identical to the Pitch & Run.

EXECUTION OF THE CHIP SHOT

The most frequently made error in the execution of The Chip Shot occurs when the golfer tries to help the ball up in the air instead of trusting the loft of the club to elevate the ball. The starting position of the Chip is extremely critical in getting you to make the shot with a descending stroke and in causing your weight to stay on your lead foot. Pay special attention to ball position, placement of the club's butt end, and shoulder alignment. In placing the butt end of the club forward of the ball by three inches, it is important that you do not open the club face to the target line as you move your hands forward. You want to be delofting the club so its leading edge stays square to the target line. As you deloft the club, you should feel the knuckles of your lead hand begin to turn a bit under the shaft, which will start to arch your wrist slightly in a bowed position. You want to maintain the bowed position during the stroke, with your knuckles staying down through the finish. The resulting feeling is the clubhead never passing the hands and no flipping of your hands and wrist. Visualize a penlight shining out of the butt end of the club, and as you stroke through the ball, the light should stay ahead of your body. If your wrist gets too active, the penlight will shine toward the middle of your body.

THE CHIP SHOT CONTINUED

ADDRESS CHIP

HANDS FORWARD

LEFT ARM RELAXED

BALL BACK

SHOULDERS LEVEL

TOP OF BACKSWING

SHOULDERS HAVE
MOVED THE ARMS

ARMS & HANDS –
MINIMAL MOVEMENT

IMPACT

BODY SHIFTS
SLIGHTLY TO LEFT

HANDS STAY
AHEAD OF CLUB

KNUCKLES
STAY DOWN

FINISH

EYES TO TARGET

CLUB CENTERED
WITH TORSO

WEIGHT TRANSFERRED
TO FRONT FOOT

THE SAND SHOT

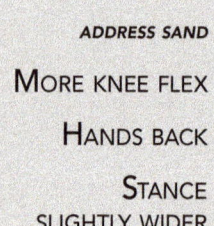

ADDRESS SAND

MORE KNEE FLEX

HANDS BACK

STANCE
SLIGHTLY WIDER

Stance – open with feet, leading edge square with intended target line, knees more flexed

Width of stance – eight to twelve inches between the heels

Butt end of the club – behind the ball by about two inches

Clubface – lofted from given loft, and also opened up about 15 degrees from square

Body center – two inches behind the ball

Weight distribution – 50/50 between the two feet

Bottom of the swing arc – two to four inches behind the ball about one inch under the sand level

Clubface contact point at impact – flange

Club selection –sand wedge

THE SAND SHOT CONTINUED

In theory, the Sand Shot should be very easy. But it remains a mystery to a majority of golfers. Many golfers don't have a good understanding of the design principles of the sand wedge itself. Once you understand the club, it is easier to make a swing that incorporates the proper use of the club. As previously mentioned, the flange of the sand wedge is below the leading edge of the club. In sand, you also open up the face of the club to the target, which sets the flange even lower in its relationship to the leading edge. In the properly executed Sand Shot, your goal is to make the back end of the club or flange skid through the sand. Historically, golfers have been told to pick up the club at a sharp angle and hit with a steep downward blow two inches behind the ball. Unfortunately, all this does is make your contact with the sand become the leading edge of the club, causing your club to become a "digger" instead of a "skidder."

EXECUTION OF THE SAND SHOT

As in the Standard Pitch and the Lob, it is necessary to let your wrist cock a little quicker so you can feel the flange can thump the sand. The club path should be swinging pretty close to parallel with your feet, and it is necessary to have your body rotating on both the backswing and forward swing. You must keep your body moving through the finish to allow your arms to extend and allow the clubhead to bottom out at its position that was preset at address. If you concentrate too hard on keeping your eyes on the ball or your head down, your body will stop, causing your arms to come up into your body too fast. This will result in many missed hits. Remember that at impact, you are trying to recreate the relationship of the clubhead and the butt end of the club with which you started at address. It is important to remember that while you are letting the flange release past your hands, you keep your body freely rotating through the ball. This allows the clubhead to accelerate and get through the sand. If you stop your body, your hands will get too "flippy" and decelerate.

THE SAND SHOT CONTINUED

ADDRESS SAND

MORE KNEE FLEX

HANDS BACK

STANCE
SLIGHTLY WIDER

TOP OF BACKSWING

BODY TURNING &
WRIST COCKING —
LETTING THE
CLUB SWING UP

THE SAND SHOT CONTINUED

IMPACT

BODY ROTATING

CLUB PASSING HANDS

FLANGE CONTACT

FINISH

PUTTING

Two elements to try to control the Putting: **Distance and Direction**.

Of these two, **distance is the most important in determining your ability to putt consistency**. When you observe amateurs, you may notice that when they practice their putting, they practice their direction. They spend a disproportionate amount of practice time on putts of less than ten feet. Once you can control your distance from far away, it is easy to control the short-range putts.

ADDRESS POSITION OF THE PUTT:

Stance – square to slightly open

Grip – thumbs straight down the shaft, very light grip pressure (hollow with the palms) and a general preference to the reverse overlap grip

Width of stance – varies with individual preference, usually five to ten inches between

Ball position – one inch forward of center

Bottom of the arc of stroke – one inch behind the ball, with the putter impacting the ball on a slight upswing

Butt end of the club – straight up and down with the clubhead

Clubface contact point at impact – bottom half of the clubface

EXECUTION OF THE PUTT

There are several universal errors in putting, starting with the attempt to control and manipulate the clubface to direct the ball toward the hole. As in the full shots, your hands should be reacting to the lead of the larger muscles. **In putting, your shoulders and**

arms are the primary *engine* of the stroke, with your hands staying very "quiet."

Another common error is attempting to hit the ball on a specific line, which leads you to start watching the roll of the ball toward the target too soon, thereby moving your head forward as you stroke through.

Putting is one area where you must keep your head motion out of the stroke. If your concentration is only on hitting the right distance, your tendency would be not to move your head but to stroke the putter with the correct pace and rhythm for the proper distance. **A good goal for your stroke is for your head and lower body (from the hips down) to remain stationary while your shoulders do the primary motion**.

Another error is the attempt to make the stroke *straight back and straight through*. This does not relate to the rest of the game because you are always trying to swing the club on an arc. The arc is on an incline because you stand to the side of the ball. As the club shaft gets longer, the plane of the arc is more horizontal. As the clubs get shorter, the arc goes more vertical. However, the USGA rules do not allow a shaft to meet the hosel of a club at more than 82 degrees. Because the ball is played away from your body, the arc will never be vertical. The only way the club could swing straight back and through would be if the stroke was traveling on a vertical plane. Therefore, your stroke should be slightly to the inside of the target line on both the backswing and through swing. Letting the club swing on its natural arc will diminish your tendency to manipulate the clubface with your hands. As you stroke on your arc, the clubface will appear to be opening and closing, but remember, the clubface is merely staying square with the arc.

There is a phrase often heard regarding putting, "Never up, never in." It gives the professionals fits to witness the amateur ram his birdie putt eight feet by the hole and hear exclaimed, "Good putt, at least you got it to the hole."

An announcer on TV made a statement in jest as an approach putt stopped short of the hole. **"Ninety-five percent of all putts left short of the hole will not go in."** Well, that statement is true, as would the statement that if you hit your ball hard enough to go four feet past the hole, it will not go in.

Ben Crenshaw made a comeback to an amateur partner in a pro am, "It is true that if you leave your putt short, it cannot go in, but you know I have never seen a ball that is past the hold go in either." Once your ball goes outside the ten-foot range, your goal is to get the ball close to the hole.

Paul Runyan once said, "If you make a twenty-foot putt, you are very lucky. However, if a golfer can hit ten putts from twenty feet and have all of them fall within a one-foot radius of the hole, the luckier they will get."

The great putters of the game – Bobby Jones, Bobby Locke, Horton Smith, Jack Nicklaus, Dave Stockton and Ben Crenshaw – are all "lag putters."

Make your goal to stop the ball *near* the hole, even if the putt is for a birdie and your partners are all pressuring you to "Make sure you get it to the hole."

If you make a twenty-foot putt, you are very lucky. However, if a golfer can hit ten putts from twenty feet and have all of them fall within a one-foot radius of the hole, the luckier they will get.

— **Paul Runyan**

DISTANCE CONTROL

Learning to control the distance of your shot is derived from an accumulation of feelings that you become accustomed to through experience and practice. It is very difficult to describe feelings. If you were asked to describe what changes you would make in the execution of pitching a penny 10 feet versus 20 feet, it would be hard to put that feeling into words. The main difference would have to be that you would move faster on the 20-foot pitch. You would not be concerned with the length of travel of your arm on the backswing. Your thoughts should be on how hard you have to throw on the forward swing. If you were asked to pitch a penny 40 feet, you would be forced to swing your arm back even farther and throw through at a quicker pace.

The same principles apply to golf and just about all sports. **The length you are going to hit a Pitch Shot is governed by two factors: 1) The length of the backswing and 2) The speed of the forward motion**. Of the two, the speed of the forward swing is more critical in determining distance. Most amateurs have poor control of their distance because that they don't use their bodies to deliver the power on the forward swing. They become so overly concerned with the ball and trying to hit it that they forget to focus on the target, which is where they want the ball to go.

A common error that amateurs make is in how they use their eyes. In the above analogy, you focus your entire energy on the wall toward which you are throwing the penny. You keep feeding the distance you have to travel into the brain and then let your body and arms do the rest. In hitting a Pitch Shot, you need to focus a great deal of your energy and eye movement on the target. You need to pay minimal attention to the ball. The only attention paid to the ball should be what kind of lie it is on. Is it uphill, downhill or sidehill, and how will that affect the ball's flight and response on the green? Watch the professionals as they prepare to hit a Pitch

Shot. Notice how many times they look at their target and how long they focus on it in their pre-shot routine. After they have a good input of target and distance, their heads return to the address, and they will perform the shot with their eyes tracking the target with the swing and ball flight.

The ability to become active in target awareness allows you to rotate easier onto a balanced position on your front foot with your eyes on the target. Trying to keep your head down will only produce "flippy" motions of the hands and arms and no resulting weight shift and rotation on the forward swing.

To control your distance, learn to use your eyes correctly, bringing the target into you. Tap the club to be secure of the bottom of the arc of your swing, and perform. Let your body rotate naturally on the backswing and forward on the through swing, and **let the ball get in the way of your motion to the TARGET**.

MYTHS OF THE GOLF SWING

Listed below are some common myths that have been perpetuated through the years. If you have any questions about them, please feel free to ask your instructor whey we consider it a myth.

Keep Your Head Down – This was explained in the Forward Swing section

Return to Your Address Position at Impact – This was explained in the Forward Swing section.

Keep Your Left Arm Straight – This causes tension in your arms. Your left arm will stay straight with the right rotation and sequence of motion on the backswing.

Start Your Backswing with Your Lead Knee Going Inward – This is a real quick way for your lead hip to go down, causing your spine to tilt toward the target, thus creating the reverse weight shift.

Swing Your Arms, Not Your Body – This causes the "dog to wag the tail," not the "tail to wag the dog." The body is the instigator of the motion. The arms and hands follow.

Stay Behind the Ball – This leads to the lower body moving forward and your shoulders going backward, which doesn't allow for weight shift on the forward swing. The result will be blocked shots to the right and quick hooks.

Transfer Your Weight to Your Rear Heel on the Backswing – This was covered under the Completion of the Backswing section.

Transfer your Weight on the Backswing by Shifting Your Hips Laterally – This was covered in Start of the Backswing section.

Hit Down on the Ball – This promotes the overuse of the arms and a downswing arc, which is too steep. The club swings on an inclined plane around the body, which is why I call it the "forward swing" instead of the "downswing."

Tuck Your Right Arm Down and Close to Your Side at Address – This causes an unnatural lowering of the right shoulder, and generally, a backswing that is too much on the inside.

GOLF IS MY GAME

The suggestion of impact is a suggestion of too much finality, for it is an integral part of this concepts of smoothness that the motion of the clubhead should not be stopped, or even impeded, as or after it strikes the ball.

Indeed, the player must always be aware that he must hit through the ball and not merely at it. He should strive for the feeling that throughout the downstroke he is continuously building up momentum until his clubhead reaches the maximum possible speed, at which point he turns the whole thing loose and allows the weight of the club and the effort of swinging to carry him along to a proper finish. A graceful, poised position at the finish of the stroke is not an end in itself, but it is, nevertheless, a very good indication of what has occurred before."

— Bobby Jones

www.ingramcontent.com/pod-product-compliance
Lightning Source LLC
Chambersburg PA
CBHW051242120626
46547CB00014B/1760